URBAN
TUMBLEWEED

Books by Harryette Mullen

Poetry

Urban Tumbleweed
Recyclopedia
Sleeping with the Dictionary
Blues Baby: Early Poems
Muse & Drudge
S*Perm**K*T
Trimmings
Tree Tall Woman

Prose

The Cracks between What We Are and
What We Are Supposed to Be:
Essays and Interviews

URBAN TUMBLEWEED

Notes from a Tanka Diary

Harryette Mullen

Graywolf Press

This publication is made possible, in part, by the voters of Minnesota through a Minnesota State Arts Board Operating Support grant, thanks to a legislative appropriation from the arts and cultural heritage fund, and through grants from the National Endowment for the Arts and the Wells Fargo Foundation Minnesota. Significant support has also been provided by Target, the McKnight Foundation, Amazon.com, and other generous contributions from foundations, corporations, and individuals. To these organizations and individuals we offer our heartfelt thanks.

Published by Graywolf Press
212 Third Avenue North, Suite 485
Minneapolis, Minnesota 55401

www.graywolfpress.org

Published in the United States of America

ISBN 978-1-55597-656-9

6 8 10 12 11 9 7 5

Library of Congress Control Number: 2013939552

Cover design: Kyle G. Hunter

Cover photo: David Schalliol, *Urban Tumbleweed*

URBAN
TUMBLEWEED

On Starting a Tanka Diary

My tanka diary began with a desire to strengthen a sensible habit by linking it to a pleasurable activity. I wanted to incorporate into my life a daily practice of walking and writing poetry. As committed as I am to writing, I needed a break in my routine, so I determined to alter my sedentary, unconsciously cramped posture as a writer habitually working indoors despite living here in "sunny California." With a pen and notebook tucked into my pocket, I could escape from the writer's self-imposed confinement, if only to walk from home to the local post office. With the tanka diary to focus my attention, a pedestrian stroll might result in a poem. Merging my wish to write poetry every day with a willingness to step outdoors, my hope was that each exercise would support the other.

Now I look forward to this daily reminder that head and body are connected. Most days I go for short walks in various parts of Los Angeles, Venice, and Santa Monica, or longer hikes in the canyons on weekends with friends. I also lead student poets on "tanka walks" in the Mildred E. Mathias Botanical Garden on the campus of UCLA. At other times I explore unfamiliar neighborhoods as I travel. Trips to the botanical garden are opportunities for learning the names of plants from all over the world that have found a home here in California, a place defined as much by non-native as by its native species.

Like many inhabitants of Los Angeles, I am not native to this state of elemental seasons: wind, fire, flood, mud-slide, and earthquake. Like ice plant, eucalyptus, and nearly all of LA's iconic palm trees, I too am a transplant to this metropolis of motor vehicles with drivers who regard, and are regarded by, pedestrians and cyclists as road hazards. Walking instead of driving allows a different kind of attention to surroundings. Each outing, however brief, becomes an occasion for reflection. Los Angeles, however urban, offers everyday encounters with nature.

So I began the diary despite being able to recognize only the most common creatures, and feeling that I lack a proper lexicon to write about the natural world, when what we call natural or native is more than ever open to question. I did not turn into an amateur naturalist or avid birdwatcher, but I became a bit more aware of my environs. The 366 tanka verses collected here represent a year and a day of walking and writing.

This is a record of meditations and migrations across the diverse terrain of southern California's urban, suburban, and rural communities, its mountains, deserts, ocean, and beaches. In greater Los Angeles my walks can range from downtown streets and alleys to spectacular natural land-scapes to outdoor shopping malls. Also noted are differences of climate and geography as I travel to other states. Parts of the tanka diary were written during a month-long residency in Marfa, Texas, sponsored by the Lannan Foundation. Others were written during a visit to Sweden where I was invited to participate in Världspoesidagen, Stockholm's celebration of World Poetry Day.

This work is my adaptation of a traditional form of Japanese syllabic verse. A tanka is a brief poem of thirty-one syllables, originally printed as a single line of text. The line is subject to internal division of semantic and syllabic units. When written in English it is customary to break the tanka into five lines, approximating its fixed pattern of syllables (5-7-5-7-7). My limited knowledge of the form is based on reading translations of a few classical and modern Japanese poets, along with contemporary tanka composed in English.

While embracing the notational spirit of this tradition, I depart from established convention in both languages, choosing instead a flexible three-line form with a variable number of syllables per line. I try to adhere to the thirty-one-syllable limit, although I am aware that the number of syllables in a given word can vary, depending on the speaker and the circumstances. "California," for example, sometimes has four syllables, at other times, five.

The brevity and clarity of tanka make it suitable for capturing in concise form the ephemera of everyday life. With refined awareness of seasonal changes and a classical repertoire of fleeting impressions, Japanese traditional poetry contemplates, among other things, the human being's place in the natural world, an idea I wanted to explore in my own nontraditional way.

What is natural about being human? What to make of a city dweller taking a "nature walk" in a public park while listening to a podcast with ear-bud headphones? What of a poet who does not know the proper names of native and non-native fauna and flora, who sees "a yellow flower by the creek"—not a *Mimulus?*

H. M.

Keep straight down this block,

then turn right where you will find

a peach tree blooming

Richard Wright

Look about you. Take hold of the things that

are here. Let them talk to you.

George Washington Carver

The morning news landed in the driveway, folded,
rolled, and rubber-banded, wrapped in plastic
for protection from the morning dews.

By midday the ardent sun burns through
the chilly morning fog and cloudy haze that weather
reporters call "May gray" and "June gloom."

Wear hat and sunglasses. Dress in layers. Peel off
clothing from morning to high noon. Put shirt
and jacket back on after sundown.

Instead of scanning newspaper headlines,

I spend the morning reading names

of flowers and trees in the botanical garden.

Each sweeping branch of California buckeye

extends a wide green hand,

presenting to the air a feathery white bouquet.

Flowers of evergreen tree called bottlebrush,

not stiff bristles but velvety filaments,

leave fingers brushed with yellow pollen.

Did early settlers risk brewing a deadly
cup of mud when they roasted and boiled
bitter seeds of the Kentucky coffee tree?

Blackfoot daisy's dark foliage withstands extreme
heat and drought, with bright-eyed flowers
that bloom almost year-round.

Flame tree, I must have missed your season
of fire. All I see are your ashy knees, your kindling
limbs, branches of extinguished blossoms.

Purple jacaranda blooms, spectacular

on branches overhead. Underfoot,

a sticky mess where they land on the sidewalk.

Awakened too early on Saturday morning

by the song of a mockingbird

imitating my clock-radio alarm.

Folded cardboard tent-shaped trap

hanging among dark leaves of the lemon tree

to capture the galling Mediterranean fly.

Chain-link fence, locked gate protect this urban
garden. Fugitive fragrance of honeysuckle
escapes to tempt the passing stranger.

Bird of paradise, a potted plant in
florist shop windows. Here in my yard
it grows with no help from me, and a head taller.

Why should I care about my neighbor's
riotous dandelions? Does he concern himself
with my slovenly jacaranda?

Walking along the green path with buds

in my ears, too engrossed in the morning news

to listen to the stillness of the garden.

Shy extrovert entices and repels

with petals and thorns. Modest exhibitionist

hides her blush under a pink ruffle.

Even in this landscaped paradise

people buy fresh-cut flowers, considered

more aesthetic than the ones growing in the yard.

As parents and children enjoy the park,

a toddler offering bread crumbs to pigeons

turns and runs as the fierce-eyed birds approach.

Shady eucalyptus grove where sleeping

butterflies cover each limb of every tree—

a rest stop on their migratory flight.

We'd planned to hike to the top of the trail

for a breathtaking view of Pacific,

but turned back down at the sight of a rattler.

Paparazzi snap snoozing celebrities

in stretch limos cruising down Hollywood

Boulevard past anorexic palm trees.

Between train station and high-rises,

he diverts pedestrians, drumming on

plastic buckets and battered metal canisters.

"No hay de queso?" a customer asks la señora

selling foil-wrapped homemade tamales

to workers waiting for the bus.

Gazing up at the city's hanging gardens:

concrete walls of freeway overpasses

with overgrown fringes of tangled vines.

Music pounds so boldly through their speakers

we all hear the beat. They're having a blast

and blasting it to everyone in earshot.

A bruised banana peel, tossed, sprawled out

on the sidewalk—what's so funny about that?

If someone slipped and fell, who would be laughing?

Pedestrians on neighborhood sidewalks,

swerving slightly to avoid smearing a child's

exuberant drawings in colored chalk.

For "curb appeal," neighbors hired a crew

of turf installers; in only two days of labor

they laid down an impressive green lawn.

If you must keep a dog in the city, you've got to go

out for walks. If you must stop

at my house, please pick up your pooch's poop.

With daily commuters, an extra passenger
on the bus. Ladybug clinging to the window
didn't need to pay a fare.

From a distance, wrecked cars on the freeway
are crumpled toys, the helicopter
circling up above, a curious dragonfly.

Parking in front of the apartment block,
the produce-truck driver whose horn announces
his arrival with "La Cucaracha."

Looking up at the sky to estimate

my mood, as if to calculate the sum

of all clouds subtracted from the total blue.

Bare feet at ocean's edge of dark, wet sand

run toward, then away from frothy waves

as small birds feed on invisible insects.

On the beach-house deck we sat at sunset

to watch the blazing Frisbee fall into the ocean

without a splash or a sizzle.

Networks of tree roots, sinewy tentacles

cracking sidewalks, pushing up bulges

in asphalt streets, clogging city sewer lines.

Along the roadside, someone has spilled

pink Styrofoam peanuts. They add color

to the grassy green, but I still prefer flowers.

A noisy crowd gathers every afternoon.

Crows on the roof, in the trees, on the lawn,

all with exciting news to crow about.

Remember summers loafing in a hammock

between two trees while a citronella coil

burns itself into an ashen snake?

Orange and yellow marigold flowers

manufacture a natural insect repellant.

In sweltering heat, you smell it.

Families avoid the beaches after heavy rains.

Swimmers stay away from the waves.

Our city gutters drain to the ocean.

For the middle of July in a drought-stricken

year, more than a few lawns in the neighborhood

are looking incredibly green.

Squirrel, stretching yourself out flat

to cool your belly on a shaded rock. On hot days

do you wish your fur coat had a zipper?

That painful summer heat of August when you burn

your hand grasping the metal doorknob

at the entrance of a house facing west.

Ferny leaf with fragrant, pink, silky fluff shades

their café patio table. Their words

mix together like citrus and champagne.

Blast of hellish breath, infernal scourge,

parched wind that whips and scorches. Green

torches, oily eucalyptus trees, bursting into flame.

Pilots drop tons of water and fire

retardant on two-hundred-foot flames

engulfing juniper, oak, and ponderosa pine.

Diminutive green-gold fans, wavering

with the faintest breeze, each languid leaf

of the gingko tree lets me feel a bit cooler.

Instead of seeing stars in the sky at night,

look for bold city lights and celestial bodies

posed on Hollywood sidewalks.

No tree in sight to shade us from the searing

glare, that cloudless day in Chinatown,

you stopped to buy a paper parasol.

Clean dirt marks the path, lined with white

stones, winding through the well-tended park,

leading to a rippling stream created for our pleasure.

The determination of a turtle

clambering out of a pond, up the slippery

side of a rock to rest in the sun.

Found on my walk today, rumpled greenbacks

dropped under a tree will reimburse me

for crisp dollars that I lost another day.

Bamboo, jointed like my finger, pointed at the sky.

What fine fishing poles you'd make for the girl

who spent hours dreaming at the lake.

Like a firefly, a charming erratic friend,

delightful to see, yet you wouldn't

depend on it for reading the newspaper.

Two seagulls face off in the parking lot

between Costco and In-N-Out,

quarreling over a half-eaten hamburger bun.

Hiking up Topanga Canyon trail,

we spoke of bobcats, coyotes, and rattlesnakes—

but only harmless lizards crossed our path.

Yes, it is legal to harvest the overhanging fruit

of your neighbor's avocado tree.

Just don't smuggle it out of state.

If I could hold this bowl of blue to cracked

lips, if to quench this desert thirst

I could swallow the sky, would I choke on carbon clouds?

Don't need picket fences, brick wall,

or razor wire. Our home's protected by

prickly pear cactus and thorny bougainvillea.

Native or not, you're welcome in our gardens.

Lavender's dress is not so vibrant as your

green trousers and purple velour sleeves.

Although they grow best in sunny places

with moist but well-drained earth, daylilies

are tolerant of many conditions and soils.

In high-school biology class my

laboratory partner took apart the frog

while I observed and took accurate notes.

Water trickles down on clean white flower,

star of five petals sheltered under green leaves

held up like cupped hands to catch the raindrops.

My visitor from Nebraska buys

a sack of assorted seashells at a souvenir shop,

then scatters them along the beach.

They steal from city streets, sell to metal recyclers

anything from bronze statues to street lamps,

fire hydrants, and manhole covers.

All water is recycled—though "toilet to tap"

was an unfortunate slogan for

the municipal water-treatment plant.

I have shamelessly neglected all of the succulent

jades and aloes you planted around the patio—

and they have thrived.

Honeybees delve in, their tailpipes

tipping up into view as their heads disappear

into the fluff of cheerfully red pompoms.

Before it was known as recycling, they were

making huarache sandals with thick black

rubber soles fashioned from reused tire treads.

A profusion of oleanders—to beautify

the freeway and filter the air, though

leaf, stem, and blossom all are poison.

Los Angeles isn't always this smoggy, you know.

There are days the sky is so clear

you can see the HOLLYWOOD sign from here.

My reckless shadow, landing on the twelve-lane

freeway down below this pedestrian bridge,

playing chicken with oncoming cars.

On the commuter train, using her camera

phone instead of a mirror, she draws

on her lips a "sinfully scarlet" smile.

Four brisk legs scissor-walking into the garden:
a quick black cat cutting through straight green
stems and folded leaves of blank white tulips.

Hummingbird alters its course, zooming
closer to check out the giant hibiscus flower—
only me in my red summer dress.

Dark-centered petals, purple coneflower,
tall parasol for fuzzy soft lamb's ear
and green-silvery stalks of dusty miller.

Here we have neighborhoods where apricot,

fig, and citrus trees are grown for show, where ripe

to bursting fruit is left to drop and rot.

> When you complain about the worm
>
> in your salad bowl, our server assures us,
>
> "That is how you know the lettuce is organic."

Those many years ago I imagined green hair

of fir tree, handshake of friendly palm,

melancholy tears of weeping willow.

In my room at El Bonito, nicknamed

"Elbow," what a previous guest left behind

resembles a different body part.

"No, thanks," she said when he offered

a sip from his flask. "You'd look good

in a bikini," he told her as she waited for the bus.

I'm not homeless. I'm a bum. I was living

in luxury, making plenty money.

But I gave it all up for alcohol.

Encyclopedia set with a few missing

volumes, snaggleteeth in enormous

jaws of a prehistoric fossil shark.

Sirens in the distance, voices of

two men arguing, the unmistakable sound

of someone vomiting in the alley.

Office memos send notice of ants invading

the sugar bowl kept in the coffee-break room,

lost bees swarming in the stairwell.

A Venice Beach sculptor caresses

wet sand to make a shapely mermaid.

He charges each tourist a fee to take her picture.

Seafood restaurants called Something's Fishy

and Killer Shrimp. An actor wearing

a frog costume waves a sign for Ugly Sushi.

Would have said this purple clustered flower

looks like a burst of fireworks, but of course it's

the fireworks that imitate the flower.

Throughout the year we exist in dazzling drought.

When the rare cloudburst occurs, we complain

about getting caught and drenched in the rain.

Adorned with snakes around his neck

like jewelry, he knows that the most beautiful

reptiles are not always the most venomous.

On Santa Monica's beach they're worshipping

a different saint. Wading in white, the chanters

launch small boats with gifts for Yemanjá.

Urban tumbleweed, some people call it,

discarded plastic bag we see in every city

blown down the street with vagrant wind.

Long ago, meat fell off the bones, animal

simmered in broth or stew of primordial

ooze, skeleton of woolly mammoth.

Non-native ice plant on postage stamps

represents the golden state like a governor

whose tongue gets tangled in California.

Paramedics check vital signs as

emergency-room doctors prepare for

the arrival of amateur mycologists.

Often they are immigrants, who've gathered,

cooked, and eaten toxic death-caps resembling

tasty wild mushrooms of their native land.

Within a small family of survivors

the cost of a grandparent's funeral

is divided between two credit cards.

Lovers of nature, when you're wandering

in the pathless wilderness and you meet

a grizzly bear, don't insist on shaking hands.

We sit still in the parked car, enchanted

to see among landscaped flowers a brown

hummingbird spangled with iridescent green.

Feeding on a single weed, its habitat

dwindling, can the caterpillar afford to be

so choosy with its appetite?

Several species of elegant butterflies

are known to be attracted to mountains

of dung and decomposing garbage.

As if they might be learning a new dance,

elders plant their feet on steady ground,

gathering wind in their arms to move cloud hands.

They shook lower branches of the tree

to loosen the tight fruit, back in those days when

they could not wait for hard green plums to ripen.

On a perfect afternoon for puppet theater

in the park, the children laugh, cheer,

and sing along with monkey and zebra.

Plastic flamingo with spinning whirligig

wings, backstroking in a stiff wind;

standing up but going nowhere fast, in reverse.

With the click of a mouse you sent me

a picture you got from someone who thought

you'd like a picture of a cat clicking a mouse.

A cop guards the bridge I cross to catch
my bus. He watches as I slow my walk
to stare at the president's car passing below.

Self-guided missile striking its target in the eye:
bee landing in the buttery yellow
center of creamy white petals.

Go ahead and pat me down with human
hands. Don't put me through that machine
with remote controls for electronic strip searches.

Until they crossed the country to that place

of rigid cold, they didn't know cascades

and tumbling waterfalls could freeze in mid-flow.

Turning suddenly, the man walking ahead

caught me staring at his pants that looked

as if he must have put them on backward.

It merely looks bedraggled, that gangling garden

of rogue roses with stems untrimmed.

It doesn't stir the heart like a true wild rose.

I can't help feeling at war with the elements,

under this fierce onslaught of rain,

with just a sad umbrella as sword and shield.

Not falling into infinite night of stars, but marks

of a black pencil, sketching dimensions,

depths, and shades of moody darkness.

With essential ingredients of air, fuel,

and spark, someone who can build a blazing

fire will always have a source of warmth.

A flurry begins with a solitary snowflake

drifting down reluctantly,

as if afraid to fall alone to earth.

Pine tops, holly berries, boxwood growing

outdoors. An everlasting aluminum tree

with puffs of spun snow displayed indoors.

Figures inside a snow globe, unperturbed

by the blizzard, feet planted firmly, no matter

how they're shaken and turned upside down.

A crack of thunder wakes me in the night,

and now, with a blanket pulled over my head,

I listen to raindrops striking the roof.

Wet and swollen after weeks of steady rainfall,

slick with slime and mold, so on wooden stairs

the visitor slipped and broke her foot.

How does a cold, faraway moon

regulate the implacable tides? Why does

a deep blue devil stand between me and the sea?

Returning home tonight, I avoid crushing

a snail that casts a scant shadow

on the wide sidewalk in clear light of a full moon.

Dried lima beans I had left soaking

to cook the next day, forgotten until

a few days later when they had started to sprout.

Storm clouds, ozone, grumble of thunder.

Lightning strike, power surge, electrical outage.

Pitch black, candle flame.

Wracked landscape of writhing worms,

a field of white grass in billowing wind. Think

of the whale's skeleton wrapped in a polar bear coat.

Even the chilliest winter day

at Santa Monica beach is still warm enough

for surfers in wet suits to hug the waves.

The fury of the storm uprooted a venerable

pine tree on the neighbors' lot

and shoved it into the roof of their house.

These colorful little stucco houses in
Sunkist Park don't look so bright today
beneath this overcast sky of cloudy gray.

A shivering dog left out in the rain,
dripping wet and cold as a miserable
werewolf, each raindrop a silver bullet.

Though they can't help flaunting their
vulnerability, I imagine that creeping snails
are trusting me to spare their fragile shells.

We're jerked awake as helicopter blades beat air.

Light glares from above. An amplified shout

orders a fleeing suspect to halt.

My usual half-hour bus ride to work took

two hours today because the president

returned for another fundraiser.

Technological worker bees patrol relentlessly,

chase and sting the enemy, while skilled beekeepers

never leave the nest.

Snippets of fresh green herbs from
a kitchen garden enhance the reputation
of the cook who makes a simple omelet.

Handcrafted pasta on the menu
has a sauce made with hen of the woods—
mushrooms that herbalists use to resist infection.

So light and delicate, skimming tips
of maidenhair trees. I thought you were butterflies.
Now I see you are the tiniest birds.

In my hotel room in Columbus, Ohio,

an arrangement of flowering weeds

plucked from the Olentangy River Trail.

At the entrance to the botanical garden,

a sign hung on the gate forewarns: "Slow down.

Watch for turtles on the roads and paths."

Their celebration of spring begins

when the festival's fresh princess is crowned

with a circlet of newly picked asparagus.

If you are perfectly still when it hovers near,

you'll hear it hum; small engine with rapid

wings, a bird no bigger than your thumb.

Waiting for the bus, a girl with plush pink

rabbit ears to match her spring outfit—

not sure what kind of bunny she's supposed to be.

Shabby (never chic) sofa hauled out

to the curb for trash when he noticed its stains

are indelible and it smells like a dog's bed.

Whiff of just-cut young grass, notes of spring

with bracing citrus, distilled and bottled

to create the designer's signature fragrance.

Because of the drizzling rain, you listened

to the sound of the wind. There, for a brief moment,

you found shelter under boughs of pines.

As one beauty encounters another, how lovely

to see the butterfly powder itself

with the flower's dusty pollen.

Grape-sized, egg-shaped, orange-colored citrus:
how strange, at first, eating whole tart-sweet fruit
with thin skin and all, biting into a kumquat.

Never as audacious as the squirrels
that sit up and beg for buttered popcorn,
the chipmunks are so shy we rarely see them.

Clicking through images downloaded
from your camera. Those buskers haven't finished
playing, and already they're in your archive.

Very late in the spring, after every living

bush and shrub had bloomed, you finally found

the strength to display a few green leaves.

Deferential to the stern blustering wind,

slender blades of grass and pliant stalks

of flowers, bowing their heads in its presence.

I wonder who left this scruffy old teddy bear

wedged between bars of a metal fence,

looking as if it's breaking out of jail.

This curly cloud don't grow straight or need
straightening. It takes rough wind to wreck the 'do.
To some, when brushed and combed it still looks tangled.

You could say I am borrowing light
from the moon when I write my tanka
after reading translations of Princess Shikishi.

Enjoying the lingering sweet-tingling
scent, I don't wash my hands right away
after peeling and eating a thick juicy orange.

Jogging along the avenue with sporty

baby strollers, they are lean and sleek in

spandex pants, proving themselves fit parents.

Suddenly orchids in bloom

no longer were rare exotic luxuries,

but sold at tempting prices in the corner market.

I leave traces of ink on paper. Others

can't resist spray-painting a boulder

or carving their names in the skin of a tree.

Contemplate layered petals of a rose

until the rapture begins. Meditate on the lotus

from now until nirvana.

Gang of Buddhist monks in the crosswalk

as yellow turns red—saffron and pomegranate

robes with running shoes and rugged sandals.

Yesterday we talked about your favorite

poem. Today you brought a gift

of fully ripe persimmons in a paper bag.

Tasting artisan chocolates,

hard to choose between Shangri-La

with goji berries or Aztec flavored with smoky chilies.

If heavenly angels want glorious instruments

to announce their arrival, they may pluck them

from the golden trumpet tree.

With all the appealing spaces on

a university campus, I wonder why

they chose this dull spot for their daily prayers.

I follow the bloody red footprints back

to their source—casual mayhem of smashed

ketchup packets smearing the gritty sidewalk.

On Venice Boulevard, men selling oranges,

women selling flowers—vendors wilting

in the sun, sweating out pungent juices.

Looking as if they might be crying,

drivers traveling west at sunset, squinting

because they have forgotten their dark glasses.

We smell rain coming, see dark clouds

and lightning before we hear thunder, watch

storms arrive, wait to get wet before running indoors.

It was no joke, but a question of survival—

the jay-walking rooster, a chicken

crossing the road in rush-hour traffic.

Do they lie down still in soft grass

to gaze up at a sky of roaming shape-shifting

clouds? Do children still have time for daydreaming?

Dried-out snake on the road

I brought as a curiosity to the child—

who insisted we give it a proper funeral.

I go for weeks without eating meat,

but sniffing the smoky aroma of barbecued ribs,

I revert back to carnivore.

Alcohol cleans tar from flip-flops. Peanut butter gets

chewing gum out of your hair. Tomato juice

rinses the stink of a skunk.

"Where does California's produce go?"

shoppers ask in supermarkets stocked

with Mexican avocados and Chinese garlic.

Alluring flesh with soft downy skin

that tickles and teases. Sun-warmed cheek

of tawny peach entices you to taste its sweetness.

On the porch, serenaded by a cricket choir—

so charming! Lying in bed, the chirp

of a single cricket—so annoying!

Ninety-nine dashing dots crisscross

the walk, red ants converging on a spot where

someone's dropped a greasy bite of pepperoni.

We keep heating up, so if we're about

to reach our melting point, this could be

the tip of the iceberg that brings us to a boil.

The fence surrounding our family garden

saves lettuce and carrots from hungry

rabbits who like salad as much as we do.

A story from my mother's girlhood:

dining with friends, she asked for her favorite

piece of chicken, was told, "Rabbits don't have wings."

Mom grew these leafy collards in her organic

garden. She picked them this morning.

Tonight they go well with our cornbread and yams.

She wonders why that misled redheaded

woodpecker keeps flying back to tap-tap-tap

on her house with aluminum siding.

The rental house transformed into enchanted cottage,

its entry way shaded with sinuous vines

of giant honeysuckle.

Upside-down reflection on the pond's

clear surface that I saw before noticing

the deer itself, camouflaged in muffled woods.

Winking fireflies never would compare themselves

to stars and galaxies. Each luminous creation

is stellar in its own realm.

Aloe vera plant in sunny kitchen window,
cool and soothing first-aid treatment
for scorched fingers of an absent-minded cook.

One thing after another: a tired old tree
topples over in the yard, turning on
the water faucet and flooding the lawn.

We awoke to their racket. Tough guys in the alley
fighting over the spoils. Then one raccoon
chased the other out to the street.

We judge the clarity of your eye and press

our fingers against your flesh to guess how long

it's been since you were pulled from the sea.

I managed to do it only that one time when

my grandfather taught me how to bait a fish hook

with a squirming wet earthworm.

Baby ducklings trailing mother duck

can scarcely wet their feet in shallow puddles

of this city's concrete rivers and creeks.

Having lost count of all our risings

and settings, we're now unable to remember

how many times we've saluted the sun.

Summer sparks, lifted up from yellowing

grass, scattered by wind. Flying up to higher

branches of pine trees, cardinals alight.

As each day becomes briefer, each night's darkness

lingers longer, we savor the deep-blushing flesh

and wine-red juice of blood oranges.

Several gallons of chemicals from the hotel pool

get poured through the wrong grate,

sickening a crowd of subway commuters.

A bobcat walked into a bar, wandered

into a saloon, entered a drinking

establishment. Everyone else skedaddled.

Clinics displaying the five-leaf marijuana plant,

weeds sprouting up more numerous than

coffee shops with the mermaid logo.

A corpulent cigar lit up in a blaze of
Old Glory—what patriotic product
is the zeppelin advertising?

Today I give thanks for grace and mercy
bestowed upon me as I go on living,
like a turkey the president pardoned.

Airline passenger detained was no
fanatic hiding explosives, but a smuggler
with expensive lizards in his pants.

Avoid brittle, dried goosefoot sold in packets

in grocery stores. Search for fresh epazote

at the outdoor farmers markets.

            Jagged leaf, used by Mexican cooks

            to flavor beans and combat flatulence;

            in large doses epazote is poisonous.

The space station smelled nothing like

an alpine mountain forest or a country meadow,

but those were places he traveled in his dreams.

I'm scanning the path, wary of poison oak

and tangled roots, but also looking

to find a simple treasure: a heart-shaped stone.

Along a familiar hiking trail I recognize

agave, sage, the summer-blooming yucca,

and sticky monkey flower.

The day I notice, returning from my walk,

a hole worn through the heel of one sock,

my thoughtful sister has sent me a new pair.

I'm seeing lots of dead zebras lately

on floors of elegant homes pictured in

interior-decorator magazines.

Pilots are grounded. Airplanes are afraid

to fly. What saboteur hid the fatal trees?

What terrorist slept beneath the glacier?

Volcanic ash clouds give a glimpse of

a possible future when no jet planes will fly,

except in emergencies such as war.

Inspired by swarms of oily insects: "If you
can't beat them, eat them," said the inventive
chef who created the locust pizza.

Shared liver of conjoined twins,

chemically preserved in a specimen jar,

in a museum of medical oddities.

Teams of ingenious student engineers
compete annually to design, build, and launch
the most seaworthy concrete canoe.

In the charming ruins of this rock-walled castle,

we could play chess with pebbles while listening

to the sparrows in Shakespeare's garden.

Ambling across the stone bridge over

a still pond covered with green skim,

I knew I would find no quieter place to be alone.

Lavender honey melts in boiling water.

Together they release unfolded flavors

of dried leaves and flowers in my cup.

Shallowest grave for the squirrel, lying still
at the foot of a tree, where I gathered leaves
to cover that small broken body.

At the Round Top, Texas, poetry festival
I find that I can live comfortably
in a log house that's air-conditioned.

After hearing that poem from my tanka diary,
you handed me a smooth and pleasing stone
shaped like a lopsided heart.

As guests are arriving I see in a corner
of the ceiling the spider's tidy web
that mocks my attempt at housekeeping.

The list of recently discovered
zoological specimens includes a flat-
faced frogfish and a carnivorous sponge.

Our best beach days are steely-gray, cloudy
and cool. We wear our thickest sweaters and listen
to the salty crunch of boots on sand.

Something had to be done, and something

must have been done to rid the campus

of its once-booming population of feral cats.

I suppose I'd become a vegetarian

if I had to kill my food. It's been ages

since I've tried to cook a lobster.

What do we call this chimerical creature

possessing hair of a dog, rabbit foot,

shark fin, elephant tusk, and rhino horn?

No, sweet light crude oil and saltwater

don't mix well at all. What's worse, they make

a terrible toxic dressing for oysters and fish.

Bees and yellow jackets are more than

hard workers. They're also soccer fans,

filling the air with the hum of their vuvuzelas.

Envisioning a snow-capped mountain top

where glacier had melted, this determined painter

climbed up to the peak and sprayed it white.

I've lost track of the twisted tale:

the war criminal, the supermodel, and

those "dirty little stones," the uncut diamonds.

A woodchuck is consulted for the weather forecast.

In other news, an octopus predicts

the winner of a soccer match.

Incident at Hollywood and Vine: Los Angeles

City firefighters rescue man caught

under train, struck by Metro Red Line.

"Oh no, not whale meat again," the Japanese
students murmured, complaining about
their lunches in the school cafeteria.

"We proudly harvest rainwater"—a sign
in a neighbor's yard. With a deep barrel
I could humbly and thankfully harvest rain.

Poked with a fingertip, it rolls into a ball.
Crawling across your open hand,
the legs of a doodlebug tickle your palm.

Behind the science building, facing a row

of vending machines, a squirrel holding

in its paws a shiny candy wrapper.

Thigh-high in water, the woman in Sri Lanka:

"This whole road's a river, so no wonder

a crocodile's on my verandah."

As the tidal wave gathered strength,

a fisherman headed his boat out to sea,

to be flung back into life by the tsunami.

Before turning to ice, polar explorer

wrote his wife about their son:

"Get the boy interested in the natural world."

Stockholm guidebooks note, in case you were

wondering, that Svartmangatan wasn't named

for a black man, but for a man dressed in black.

White chimneys wearing stovepipe hats top

rustic red cottages, built for broom makers

and rock blasters, on steep hills of Södermalm.

Wandering lost in Stockholm's twilight streets,

at last I recognize a helpful sign:

TOMATO in the toothpaste over Slussen.

I've packed my text. They've checked the mikes.

My words unfold and now behind my back

my earthy language has become an alien tongue.

What did I bring home from Sweden?

Ham sandwich that the dog sniffed, the inspector

confiscated. Grit collected from Stockholm streets.

Thin airmail envelope with indecipherable

handwriting; I tear it open

to release an inky blue butterfly.

          A man disguised as a baggy cow

            steals twenty-six gallons of milk from Walmart,

              then gives it all to strangers outside the store.

Fourteen exotic birds, lulled asleep, bagged

and taped to the body of the smuggler

arrested in the airport customs line.

Hopeless escape, wild animal keeper

setting the captives loose in Zanesville, Ohio,

before shooting himself in the head.

        The closest we got to nature: red fruit

        floating above city skyline

        on label of two-liter bottle of Cherry Coke.

You may wrap yourself in silk pajamas

after nibbling your coverlet,

chenille caterpillar lounging on a tender leaf.

A "valet" parks your car at the supermarket.
A "beach butler" reserves your plot of sand
with folding chair and bright umbrella.

The police and health departments want
to find out who's been dumping human waste
in the streets of Venice and Santa Monica.

In early morning hours, workers with a pickup
truck make frequent stops, collecting
shopping carts left on the streets the night before.

Wet droplets falling on faces of church
congregation as the father strides down the aisle
sprinkling holy water and bless-yous.

That homeless woman who hated my shoes
last week—now she lets me buy her
a cup of her favorite mango frozen yogurt.

Stone-ground flour from co-op bulk bins
brings dusty moths that hatch in my kitchen canister
and fly out when I want to bake biscuits.

Behind crumbling walls of ruined adobe,

above radiant orange zinnias,

hummingbirds are aerial acrobats.

Neglected, lapsed in memory, declined,

dilapidated, fallen into decay,

crumbled into dust, returned to nature.

Stranger here and even more out of place

than I am, sapphire-blue peacock

promenading down Waco Street in Marfa, Texas.

A spectacular storm on the way to El Paso;

four lanes of traffic halted by

a jack-knifed truck that skidded in the rain.

A kind friend sent me a hastily scribbled note,

inquiring about my "tanka dairy."

I wrote back to say, "I'm milking it."

Along the two-lane desert highway,

solitary Joshua trees appear at regular intervals,

like posted mile markers.

Here we imagine how we might perish: by lightning

strike or snakebite, drowned in a flash or

parched and shriveled in withering heat.

We drive a borrowed car to Pueblo Market

to get our rice and pinto beans,

avocados, jalapeños, and popsicles.

Stately pedestrians, they claim the right of way

on any street, and now wild turkeys on the lawn

chase me back into the house.

Our guided tour ends with outdoor works
of the cantankerous artist; concrete boxes
set in a landscape of "Chinati beige."

A pink snake racing across the desert
hardly needs explanation, unless
you believe it is only a trick of the mind.

On one spiny paddle of the dusty cactus plant
a single yellow flower spreads its petals
for a thirsty hummingbird.

They're meant to underscore boredom or an awkward

silence: recorded cricket chorus

or desert wind rolling a tumbleweed.

It wasn't a bat. Only smudged wings of a giant

moth colliding with your face, startling

as daylight surrendered to shadows.

Had I stayed longer, I might have seen

or maybe smelled a pack of peccaries—

rank javelinas tipping through the neighborhood.

There I went, leaving only my footprints.

Returning, I brought back nothing but

the dust that clings to the sole of a wanderer.

A green streak swooshed across the sky

with a shower of brilliant blue sparks. A boulder

hurled from heaven breaking apart in earth's air.

When I am blazing ghost animated by motion

capture and you the wind inhaling words

then how on earth do you read me?

Florida's cook-off contest to popularize

recipes for lion fish, wild boar,

and python—the state's invasive species.

Why accept what nature gave us?

We're designing our own vegetables so

no regulator can make us eat broccoli.

A year after the triple disaster,

a ghost ship's crossed the Pacific,

but farmers may never return to Fukushima.

Hibernating reptiles and amphibians

awaken in spring when rattlers become

restless and turtles think of traveling.

Mother of octuplets turns down the lead role

in a porn film, but agrees to pose

"tastefully nude" for a tabloid magazine.

The size of a man's hand, covered with

warts. Alarming creatures may have beguiling

eyes, but it's hard to fall in love with a toad.

Standing his ground in a pair of elegant

leather shoes, offering each passer-by

a chance to buy the homeless newspaper.

At night our tidy-clean, green park is locked

to keep out rough sleepers who bed down on sidewalks

next to shopping carts full of rubbish.

Visiting with us in Los Angeles, our friend

went out for a sunny walk, returned

with wrists bound, misapprehended by cops.

Meandering through hill-top neighborhood

of splendid old mansions, I loiter at wrought-iron gates

picketing the senator's home.

Nothing better to do, I imagine, than try

to get back to sleep after waking

in the slack of night from a tiresome dream.

When you see me walking in the neighborhood,

stopping to admire your garden, I might be

composing a tanka in my head.

Trapped and hunted to the edge of

extinction, gone for nearly ninety years

when a lone gray wolf appears in California.

At first, the dog walker mistook it for a horror-

movie prop—that severed head found in the park,

beneath the HOLLYWOOD sign.

Gather loose strands from brush and comb;

roll them into a thick Ziggy dreadlock;

mail to an artist who collects the hair of poets.

Eerie mementos of living and dead:
vials of blood in a wooden box,
clumps and curls of hair displayed in plastic bags.

The heart of a saint, stolen from a church
in Dublin. Thieves leave golden chalices,
costly art, choosing this most priceless relic.

They stare as I peer into the window
of a junk shop—bright beady eyes of a
taxidermy wolf with mangy molting fur.

When tainted honeybees become disoriented,

lose their way, and never make it back

to the hive, their colonies collapse.

We'll lasso asteroids as they circle

the planet. We'll find a way to mine

their wealth of aluminum, gold, and platinum.

Woman waiting for a bus to work or walking

early in the morning, beware

the violent man with a teardrop tattoo.

Employees at the county landfill sift

through two weeks of dumpster trash to help

the deputies searching for thrown-away children.

It comes closer, beams brighter, seems fuller

tonight, at this point in its elliptical orbit

around our earth—the super moon.

With darkness as his accomplice,

the blind prisoner finds a way out, slipping

unseen past sentries meant to keep him out of sight.

Arcadius crashed after winning the race.

Cause of death, not drugs but aneurysm.

Vet said, "It could have happened any time."

A bird flew across the border

and when it came to rest, was suspected

of being an alien and possibly a spy.

On a stretch of beach within range

of the military base, two rocks she'd collected

ignited in the pocket of her shorts.

Couldn't prick a pinhole in heavy cover

of cloud to watch the sun, already curtained,

hide itself behind a darkened moon.

A dinosaur can fetch a hefty sum

when the most complete set of well-preserved

Tyrannosaurus bones is sold at auction.

Climbers on Everest, so fixed on reaching

their goal they press on beyond fatigue,

passing their predecessors, the frozen dead.

Confronting the suspect, police use lethal

force against a disorderly mountain

lion trespassing in a private yard.

A homeless woman spends her days collecting

odd scraps of paper, then sits in front

of the all-night drugstore, poring over them.

Within territorial boundaries of

contested city blocks, yellow fire hydrants

are marked with graffiti signatures.

In a few billion years Andromeda Galaxy

will collide with our Milky Way, but worlds

come to an end every day.

Like waterskiing in a deluge, hitching a ride

on a drop of rain is how the mosquito

survives in a downpour.

Rare event, transit of Venus, when

the planet appears as a small black dot,

a beauty mark penciled on the face of the sun.

Often I would bathe my face with saltwater

from the restless ocean. If there's water on the moon,

it must be frozen by now.

I've yet to see them in flower or bearing fruit,

these sharp brittle twigs, these scratchy

thin branches of the bony thorn-apple tree.

Unseasonably warm, and in the background

of the afternoon press conference, you can hear

mockingbirds on the White House lawn.

Computer graphic art is grooming

virtual hair and feathers of animated

creatures to obey the laws of physics.

You could survive to antiquity and die

alone like hundred-year-old tortoise

just passed away on Galápagos Islands.

After official autopsy, carefully preserved

remains of Lonesome George are bubble-wrapped,

duct-taped, and stored in a freezer.

Visiting with you that spring in Maryland,

how often I wished I could gather

those bright cherry blossoms into a tanka!

It wouldn't cost five cents or a nickel

to name as our national mammal

the bison or the American buffalo.

A local ordinance against cruelty

to geese puts an end to foie gras on

a stick wrapped in a cloud of cotton candy.

Pacific pocket mouse—somewhat less

endangered on the firing range where guns

aim at standing targets, not burrowing critters.

You can drive south from San Francisco;

I'll come up from LA. So let's meet in the middle

at that cheap but cozy beach motel.

Southern California family surprised

to discover uninvited black bear taking

a dip in their suburban pool.

Human footprints in the dust

marked the latest entry in the record

of earth's history written on the surface of the moon.

TUMBLEWEED, name in black letters

on the side of a bright yellow bus

delivering students to open gates of Windward School.

"Who do you think I am? Tippi Hedren

in an Alfred Hitchcock film?" I wondered,

when that flying object pecked me on the head.

So accustomed to minor temblors,

I woke for only a moment before turning

over in bed and going back to sleep.

As you have forgotten, so one day

might you remember how to be wild

and bewildered, to be wilder and be wilderness?

Today's technology allows scientists

to analyze the last meal of a

prehistoric insect preserved in amber.

Craving the season of spring, we hunt for

plump raspberries, fava beans, and pencil-thin

asparagus in the farmers' markets.

After all these years, when each has lost

someone we love, you still remember stopping by

to share a meal of lentil soup and bread.

It alters the mood of our calm conversation

when we have to shout to be heard

beneath the roar of jets and helicopters.

Worn by many young women on campus,

casual shorts and sleeveless tops with logo labels

that proclaim them PINK and JUICY.

The ax used to split up the furniture

of her faithless lover, on display

in the museum of broken relationships.

Several homeowners organize a neighbor-

hood watch patrol after discovering uscd

rubbers discarded on their lawns.

A young man I wouldn't notice, if not for

words overheard, not even whispered

into his phone, "Two hundred for a blow job."

Intrepid, worldly, and sophisticated food critic

laments she's found no wine pairs well

with scorpions or tarantulas.

While dreaming my way up the mountain,

I sleepwalked into my kitchen

where I slipped on a pebble, or was it a potato?

Hovering half-awake, uncertain if those

sounds were bird or child. We say that human

hatchlings coo, and so do doves and pigeons.

Random genetic tests suggest

the fish brought to your table is unlikely to be

what's written on the restaurant menu.

Later, I wonder if I heard right.

An exceptional hairdresser might have said

to a client, "Two hundred for a blow dry."

Rainy, spicy leaves of the California laurel,

scented with a hint of cardamom, like

chewing gum I used to crave.

A student's original excuse for not

turning in her homework—her life turned

inside out by an infestation of bedbugs.

Remember that song about possum up

a 'simmon tree? That's who's living in your

backyard, opossum up the persimmon tree.

Beekeepers couldn't sell the strange green

and blue honey their bees made after

snacking on candy from the M&M's factory.

Ha-ha-haw-haw, the dark bird's rowdy laughter

as it flew over the heads of earthbound

pedestrians who didn't get the joke.

In the aftermath of the tsunami,

rescuers look for survivors, find in

the arms of a tree a hungry baby boy.

"But they can't see any ocean from where
they live," the realtor laughs. "That area
could be Mar Vista in English only."

In greening spring when every leafy thing
is waking, the blanched and naked branches
of a gnarled tree look all the more desolate.

"Do you hear me?" Yes, I turn my head.
A stranger talking on the phone, "Listen to me.
Stop saying you're going to kill yourself."

Feeling rueful, seeing the FOR LEASE sign

where their shop used to be. Never went in,

except that one time with the homeless woman.

Unearthed by San Francisco construction workers,

a nugget of gold and a broken ten-inch tooth

of ice-age woolly mammoth.

For every community plot and rooftop

garden, how many seeds that sprouted in crooked

cracks, the plants that no one planted?

Zigzag legs, barbed predator claws—startling

discovery, the ancient Trogloraptor family

of large cave-dwelling spiders.

With a vigorous push of a broom,

a worker sweeps enterprising squirrel

out the front door of the natural food co-op.

The mockingbird and monarch butterfly

arrive on cue as I sit on a garden bench

to write in the tanka diary.

A scenic backdrop of young bamboo stalks

growing in a corner of the yard, inspiring

the children's tropical adventures.

Versed in country things and sensitive

to seasons, the poet knew that nature never

wept for us no matter how gently it rained.

Favorite sandals, constantly worn,

that remembered the shape of my feet—

lost in a whirlpool as I crossed the roiling water.

I'm sure I must have been laughing

the first time we hiked that mountain trail,

when you introduced me to the sticky monkey flower.

Plain colors we wear, compared to

green-shimmering wings of hummingbird

stroking opulent purple velvet of Mexican sage.

Today we found an ephemeral shrine

at the end of the trail—rocks and pebbles

some hiker had arranged to make a spiral.

In their beach-themed bungalow,

a coffee table built from a recycled

surfboard cut from a California redwood tree.

Halfway across an empty street I pause

to hear water flowing swiftly beneath

where I stand on a sturdy manhole cover.

Even itinerant tumbleweed had roots

attaching it to the land, before its stem snapped

and strong winds pushed it down the road.

Zesty greens tossed with organic virgin

olive oil and vinegar, a salad of weeds

foraged from the pristine countryside.

On a breath of air, they may last longer

and travel farther than we know,

our folded paper boats and origami airplanes.

Caught a quick glimpse of bright eyes,

yellow feathers, dark wings. Never learned your name—

and to you, bird, I also remain anonymous.

Acknowledgments

I gladly acknowledge the editors of the following publications and media projects where parts of this work appeared previously: *The Academy of American Poets Poem-A-Day Series, African American Review, Argos Books Poetry Calendar, The Baffler, Bombay Gin, Borderlands: Texas Poetry Review, Callaloo, Columbia: A Journal of Literature and Art, Court Green, Denver Quarterly, Float Press August Postcard, Gulf Coast: A Journal of Literature and Fine Arts, Hambone, Harvard Review, Iron Horse Literary Review, Lana Turner: A Journal of Poetry and Opinion, Maggy, The Neruda Project, Orion, Ploughshares, Qui Parle, Stone Canoe, University of California Press Newsletter,* and *Western Humanities Review.*

My interest in using tanka to explore the question "What is natural about being human?" might be traced to the serendipitous convergence of staying at Soul Mountain Retreat in East Haddam, Connecticut, and subsequently reading Kimiko Hahn's *The Narrow Road to the Interior* around the same time that Camille T. Dungy chose one of my poems for *Black Nature: Four Centuries of African American Nature Poetry.* In an anthology that includes haiku by Richard Wright, Dungy contests the boundaries of nature poetry as well as African American poetry, resisting typical assumptions that "green" is white and "urban" is black. Hahn, alternating tanka and zuihitsu (literary prose), creates a personal work that also is in dialogue with Matsuo Bashō, Princess Shikishi, Murasaki Shikibu, Sei Shōnagon, and other Japanese writers.

The end of my preface refers to a discussion of the poet's lexicon for describing the natural environment—yellow flower versus *Mimulus*—that occurred between Linda Gregg and Robert Hass, who mentioned their exchange to Zack Rogow in an interview about Hass's *Time and Materials*.

I wrote parts of the tanka diary in Marfa, Texas, where I was a happy guest of the Lannan Foundation. Other entries I associate with visits to Goddard College, University of Louisville, Naropa University, Ohio State University, Vermont Studio Center, and other communities and campuses where I was invited as a guest writer. A few were written during a week in Sweden where I visited Södertörn University and joined in Stockholm's celebration of World Poetry Day, sponsored by the Författarcentrum or Writers Center.

Always I am grateful for family, friends, and colleagues who walk the path with me, especially my mother and sister; my constant writer friends Wendy Belcher, Mary Bucci Bush, Ellen Krout-Hasegawa, Kathleen McHugh, and Alice Wexler; Marilyn Nelson, for the inspiration of Soul Mountain; Erica Hunt and Tonya Foster, who invited me to discuss with kindred spirits the making of this work; Mary Helen Washington, for critical perspective and lively conversation; Miriam Silverberg, for her interest in Japanese modernism; and Cal Bedient, who was the first to accept a selection from

the tanka diary for publication, encouraging me to think that
it might have a life beyond my own.

My thanks to David Schalliol for permission to use his
photograph for the cover design, and to the staff of Graywolf
Press, notably editor Jeffrey Shotts, for all their work to bring
this book into existence.

Harryette Mullen is the author of seven previous books of poetry, including *Recyclopedia* and *Sleeping with the Dictionary,* a finalist for the National Book Award, the National Book Critics Circle Award, and the *Los Angeles Times* Book Prize. She has recently received the Academy of American Poets Fellowship and the Jackson Poetry Prize from Poets & Writers. She is Professor of English and African American Studies at the University of California, Los Angeles.

Book design by Connie Kuhnz. Composition by BookMobile Design & Digital Publisher Services, Minneapolis, Minnesota. Manufactured by Versa Press on acid-free 30 percent post-consumer wastepaper.